DINO-SORTED!

FLYING (PTEROSAUR) REPTILES

CLASSIFY THE FEATURES OF PREHISTORIC CREATURES

SONYA NEWLAND

Gareth Stevens PUBLISHING

Please visit our website, www.garethstevens.com. For a free color catalog of all our high-quality books, call toll free 1-800-542-2595 or fax 1-877-542-2596.

Cataloging-in-Publication Data
Names: Newland, Sonya.

Title: Flying reptiles / Sonya Newland.
Description: Buffalo, NY : Gareth Stevens Publishing, 2026. | Series: Dino-sorted! | Includes glossary and index.
Identifiers: ISBN 9781482473605 (pbk.) | ISBN 9781482473612 (library bound) | ISBN 9781482473629 (ebook)
Subjects: LCSH: Pterosauria--Juvenile literature. | Pterosauria--Classification--Juvenile literature.
Classification: LCC QE862.P7 N483 2026 | DDC 567.918 --dc23

Published in 2026 by
Gareth Stevens Publishing
2544 Clinton St.
Buffalo, NY 14224

First published in Great Britain in 2020 by
The Watts Publishing Group

Credits
Editor: Sonya Newland
Designer: Dan Prescott, Couper Street Type Co.

The publisher would like to thank the following for permission to reproduce their pictures:

Alamy: Stocktrek Images, Inc. 14, Corbin17 19t, Melba Photo Agency 21; Shutterstock: Catmando cover, 5tr, 10, 15t, 24, 26, Linda Bucklin 4, 20–21, 22, 28–29, Warpaint 5tl, 6, 16–17, 19b, 23t, 24–25, Dariush M 5b, Dmitry Grigoriev 7t, Michael Rosskothen 7b, 9, 17, 29, Herschel Hoffmeyer 8bl, 8–9, ILYA AKINSHIN 8br, Elenarts 11t, 13t, 23b, Natalia Gorbach 11b, Valentyna Chukhlyebova 12–13, 15b, AKKHARAT JARUSILAWONG 13b, YuRi Photolife 18, njaj 27.

All design elements from Shutterstock.

Printed in the United States of America

CPSIA compliance information: Batch #CSGS26: For further information contact Gareth Stevens at 1-800-542-2595.

PRONUNCIATION GUIDE

Anhanguera (an-han-GAIR-ah)

Dimorphodon (di-MOR-fo-don)

Dorygnathus (dor-e-NAY-fus)

Dsungaripterus (sung-ah-rip-TEH-rus)

Eudimorphodon (yoo-di-MOR-fo-don)

Hatzegopteryx (hat-zeg-gop-TEH-rix)

Nemicolopterus (neh-me-co-lop-TER-us)

Peteinosaurus (peh-tain-oh-SORE-us)

Pteranodon (teh-RAN-oh-don)

Pterodactylus (teh-roh-DACK-til-us)

Quetzalcoatlus (kwet-zal-co-AT-las)

Rhamphorhynchus (RAM-foh-RINK-us)

Tapejara (tup-ay-HAR-ah)

Thalassodromeus (fah-LASS-oh-DRO-meus)

Tyrannosaurus rex (tie-RAN-oh-SORE-us recks)

Zhejiangopterus (zee-zhang-op-TEH-us)

CONTENTS

MEET THE

WHILE THE DINOSAURS ROAMED THE LAND, A DIFFERENT GROUP OF ANIMALS TOOK TO THE SKY. LIKE THE DINOSAURS, PTEROSAURS (WHICH MEANS "WINGED LIZARDS") WERE REPTILES, BUT THEY HAD MANY FEATURES THAT MADE THEM DIFFERENT FROM DINOSAURS. PTEROSAURS WERE THE FIRST VERTEBRATES TO FLY.

Eudimorphodon

Pterosaurs appeared about 225 million years ago, just after the first dinosaurs. The earliest group of pterosaurs are known as basal pterosaurs, or rhamphorhynchoids. They were characterized by long tails, short necks, and several teeth. The pterodactyloids emerged later, in the Late Jurassic Period. These pterosaurs had shorter tails, longer necks, and fewer teeth.

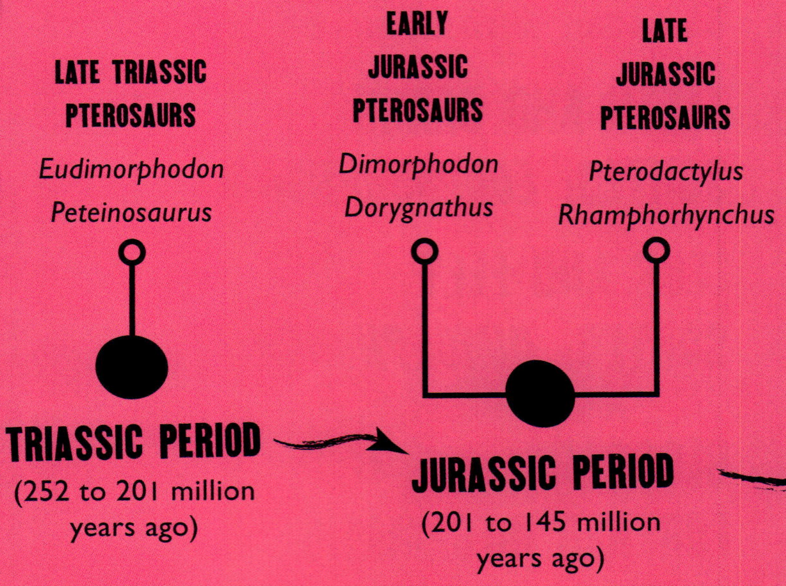

PTEROSAURS

All the pterosaurs, along with the dinosaurs, died out around 66 million years ago in a mass extinction event. Experts believe that an asteroid struck Earth in the area that is now Mexico. The impact of the asteroid threw up so much gas and dust that Earth's climate changed dramatically. Few living creatures could adapt quickly enough to survive.

EARLY CRETACEOUS PTEROSAURS

Anhanguera
Dsungaripterus
Nemicolopterus
Tapejara
Thalassodromeus

LATE CRETACEOUS PTEROSAURS

Hatzegopteryx
Pteranodon
Quetzalcoatlus
Zhejiangopterus

CRETACEOUS PERIOD
(145 to 66 million years ago)

VARIED SIZES

OVER MILLIONS OF YEARS, MORE THAN 200 SPECIES OF PTEROSAUR EXISTED ON EARTH. THEY CAME IN ALL DIFFERENT SIZES. SOME WERE SMALLER THAN A BLACKBIRD, WHILE THE LARGEST WAS THE SIZE OF A SMALL PLANE!

◀ *Peteinosaurus* was one of the smallest—and the earliest—pterosaurs. Its wingspan was about 24 inches (60 cm).

It's hard know exactly which were the smallest and largest pterosaurs. Paleontologists rely on fossil evidence to estimate sizes, and it is rare to find a complete fossil skeleton. However, *Nemicolopterus* may have been the smallest "winged lizard." This tiny pterosaur was no bigger than a sparrow!

Among the pterodactyloids is a sub-group known as azhdarchidae. Some of the largest pterosaurs belong to this group, including *Quetzalcoatlus* (see pages 8–9) and *Hatzegopteryx*. These Late Cretaceous pterosaurs were a very successful group, and their fossils have been found all over the world. In fact, they may have been the last surviving pterosaurs before the mass extinction event occurred.

Hatzegopteryx was one of the largest pterosaurs, but it had a shorter, more muscular neck than other members of its family.

Experts can only estimate how much the different pterosaurs weighed. Some of them were very big, but they may not have been heavy–otherwise they wouldn't have been able to fly!

Pterosaurs may have taken flight from all fours, using their "arms" as front legs.

SORTED:

QUETZALCOATLUS

***QUETZALCOATLUS* MAY BE THE LARGEST FLYING CREATURE TO HAVE EVER EXISTED. THIS HUGE PTEROSAUR EMERGED IN THE LATE CRETACEOUS PERIOD AND DIED OUT IN THE MASS EXTINCTION EVENT 66 MILLION YEARS AGO.**

SCAVENGER

Quetzalcoatlus probably fed mostly on fish and shellfish from the rivers and seas. Experts think it may also have been a scavenger, like a modern vulture. It flew over the land looking for dead animals, then swooped down to feast on them using its sharp beak.

DINOMIGHTY!

With a 6.5-foot (2-m) long head at the end of a 10-foot (3-m) neck, *Queztalcoatlus* was nearly as tall as a giraffe!

WINGS

With a wingspan of up to 40 feet (12 m), *Quetzalcoatlus* was a giant of the skies. For comparison, the biggest flying creature alive today is the wandering albatross—and the largest wingspan ever measured on this bird is 12 feet (3.6 m)! *Quetzalcoatlus* was so large that it may not have been able to keep flapping its wings for long periods of time. Instead, it probably glided through the air.

QUICK FACTS

PERIOD:
Late Cretaceous

LIVED IN:
North America

HEIGHT:
18 feet (5.5 m)

WINGSPAN:
40 feet (12 m)

FUR

Quetzalcoatlus means "feathered serpent." However, like other pterosaurs, *Quetzalcoatlus* didn't have feathers like a bird. It may have had fuzzy fur or hair-like scales on its body.

STRONG WINGS

PTEROSAURS WEREN'T BIRDS. THEY WEREN'T EVEN THE ANCESTORS OF MODERN BIRDS! BUT THESE REPTILES COULD FLY THANKS TO THEIR LARGE, STRONG WINGS, WHICH WERE ATTACHED TO EACH SIDE OF THEIR BODY.

◀ Pterosaurs with shorter wings could maneuver quickly, twisting and turning to catch prey in the air.

A pterosaur's wings weren't like the wings of modern birds. They were made of skin like a bat's wings. The skin of the wings was strengthened by thin strips of muscle running through it.

Pterosaurs had strong muscles in other parts of their body to help them move their wings. Muscles in the upper shoulder pulled the wings upwards. Muscles in the chest pulled the wings back down. When they were resting, pterosaurs folded their wings away by their sides.

To take off, a pterosaur would launch itself into the air from a high point with its hands and feet, and then open its wings.

As well as their wings, pterosaurs had arms, wrists, and fingers. The arm bones supported the wings. The top of the wing was attached to the very long fourth finger.

SORTED:

PTERANODON

PTERANODON WAS ONE OF THE BIGGEST PTEROSAURS. MANY FOSSILS OF THIS PREHISTORIC FLYING REPTILE HAVE BEEN FOUND, SO PALEONTOLOGISTS HAVE BEEN ABLE TO FIGURE OUT QUITE A LOT ABOUT IT.

QUICK FACTS

PERIOD:
Late Cretaceous

LIVED IN:
North America

LENGTH:
10 feet (3 m)

WINGSPAN:
23 feet (7 m)

WINGS

Pteranodon had huge wings. This meant it could glide easily, traveling a long way without wasting energy by moving its wings much. This is similar to the way many seabirds travel today. Flapping its wings would also have been difficult because *Pteranodon* was so big. This pterosaur was designed to soar!

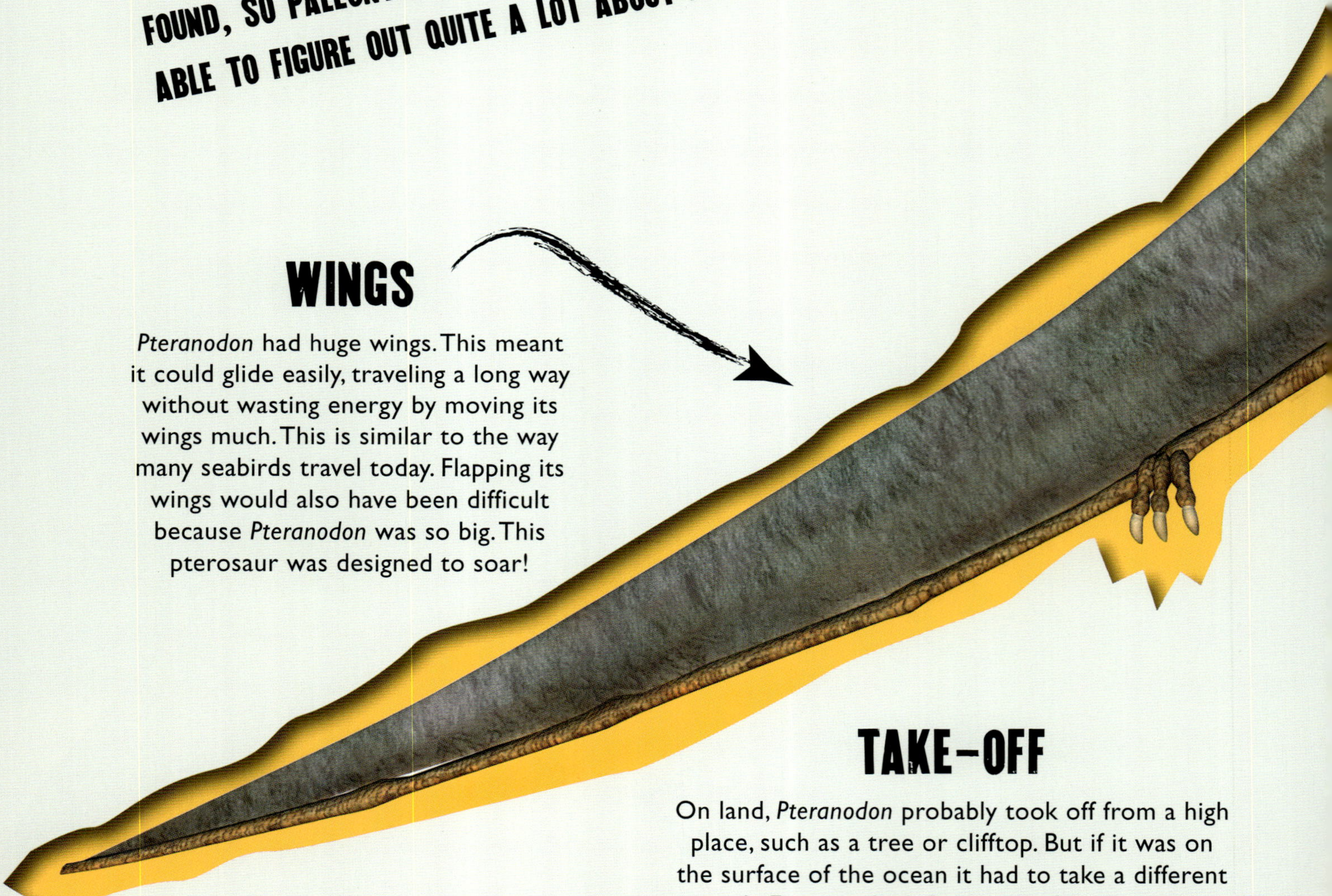

TAKE-OFF

On land, *Pteranodon* probably took off from a high place, such as a tree or clifftop. But if it was on the surface of the ocean it had to take a different approach. Experts think *Pteranodon* faced into the sea breezes with its big wings open. The wind would have provided enough lift under its wings for it to take off.

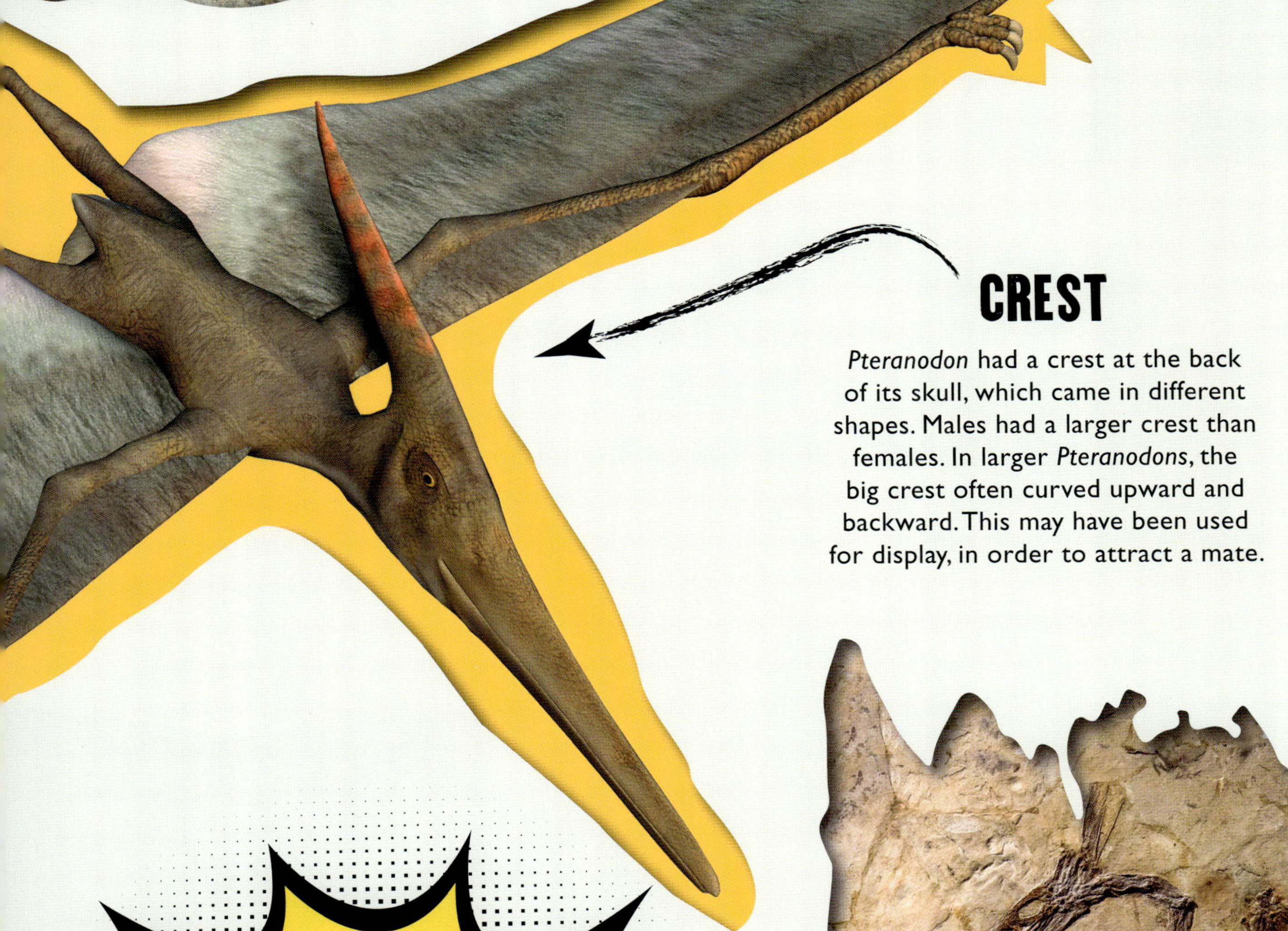

CREST

Pteranodon had a crest at the back of its skull, which came in different shapes. Males had a larger crest than females. In larger *Pteranodons*, the big crest often curved upward and backward. This may have been used for display, in order to attract a mate.

DINOMIGHTY!

Pteranodon's wings could be about as long as four adults lying top to toe!

HEADS AND TAILS

TO BALANCE THEIR WIDE WINGS, PTEROSAURS USUALLY HAD LONG SKULLS. THEIR TAILS ALSO PROVIDED STABILITY IN THE AIR. MOST BASAL PTEROSAURS HAD LONG TAILS. THE LATER PTERODACTYLOIDS HAD SHORTER TAILS.

Some pterosaurs had crests on their head. Paleontologists think these may have been used to help the reptiles steer while flying, or to keep them steady in the air. The crest may also have been colored as a way of attracting a mate.

Tapejara had a semicircular crest over its beak, which may have been a bright color as a form of display.

Pterosaurs used their tails for steering. Pterosaur tails were usually thin. Some had a flap of skin, called a vane, at the end, which could be diamond- or oval-shaped.

Paleontologists think that pterosaur tails may have helped the reptiles steer through the air, a bit like a boat's rudder.

Basal pterosaurs' tails were thin and bony. They were also quite stiff, with a more flexible section at the end. The long tails of these earlier pterosaurs had up to 50 vertebrae in them. By comparison, a *T. rex* had about 40 vertebrae in its tail.

Pterodactyloids' tails were shorter. They were made up of just a few bones– as few as 10 vertebrae. Some pterosaurs, such as *Pterodactylus*, had no tail at all. This may have made it easier for them to dart and dive in the air, like a fighter jet.

The Early Cretaceous pterodactyloid *Anhanguera* had just a tiny tail.

SORTED:

RHAMPHORHYNCHUS

QUICK FACTS

PERIOD:
Late Jurassic

LIVED IN:
Europe, Africa

LENGTH:
1.6 feet (50 cm)

WINGSPAN:
6 feet (1.8 m)

PALEONTOLOGISTS HAVE DISCOVERED SOME WELL-PRESERVED FOSSILS OF THE JURASSIC *RHAMPHORHYNCHUS*. THESE AMAZING FINDS EVEN INCLUDE WING MEMBRANES AND THE VANE AT THE END OF THE PTEROSAUR'S TAIL.

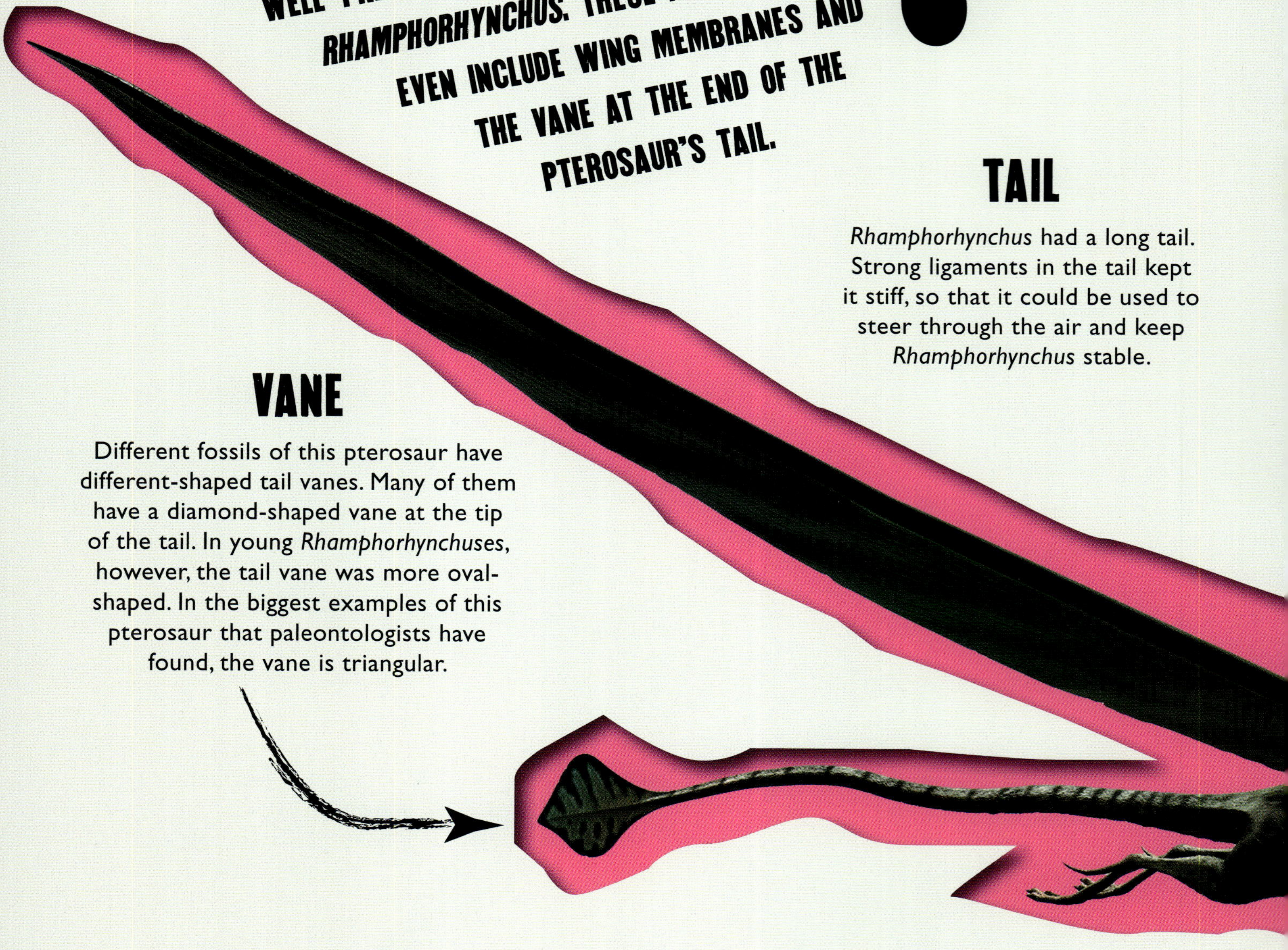

TAIL

Rhamphorhynchus had a long tail. Strong ligaments in the tail kept it stiff, so that it could be used to steer through the air and keep *Rhamphorhynchus* stable.

VANE

Different fossils of this pterosaur have different-shaped tail vanes. Many of them have a diamond-shaped vane at the tip of the tail. In young *Rhamphorhynchuses*, however, the tail vane was more oval-shaped. In the biggest examples of this pterosaur that paleontologists have found, the vane is triangular.

DINOMIGHTY!

Rhamphorhynchus may have been able to swim! It probably dived under the water and hunted for fish below the surface, using its wide feet to propel itself.

HEAD

Rhamphorhynchus had a long skull. Its teeth pointed forward at an angle and were arranged in a way that formed a kind of mesh when the jaw was closed. This would have created an effective "cage" to trap fish. The tip of the jaw was beak-like, with no teeth in it.

HOLLOW BONES

MANY PTEROSAURS SEEM TOO BIG AND AWKWARD TO BE BUILT FOR FLYING. THE BIGGER AN ANIMAL IS, THE HARDER IT IS FOR IT TO TAKE OFF. SO HOW DID THE PTEROSAURS DO IT? THE SECRET TO THEIR FLYING SUCCESS WAS IN THEIR BONES.

The pteroid bones at the top of a pterosaur's wings supported the wing membrane. They ran from the wrist to the shoulder. No other flying creature has this bone.

The pterosaurs had air sacs in their bones. These hollow areas kept the weight of the reptiles down even when they grew to huge sizes. The bones were crisscrossed with small bony rods to strengthen them. Hollow bones are something they share with modern birds.

Most pterosaurs had a large skull. Holes for the nasal passages and at the front of the eye sockets joined together to make larger holes. This lightened the skull so the head wasn't too heavy to lift or fly with.

The large holes in this *Quetzalcoatlus* (see pages 8–9) skull were not just the eye sockets. They were also the nasal passages.

Thalassodromeus had one of the largest skulls of any pterosaur, with an ornate crest.

The wing bones were also hollow, with very thin walls. Unfortunately, this made the bones very fragile, so when they became fossils in the ground, they were crushed easily. It's hard to find well-preserved pterosaur bones.

SORTED:

ANHANGUERA

THIS EARLY CRETACEOUS PTEROSAUR IS ONE OF THE BEST-KNOWN. FOSSILS OF PREHISTORIC REPTILES LIKE THIS HAVE HELPED PALEONTOLOGISTS UNDERSTAND HOW THEIR BONE STRUCTURE ALLOWED LARGE PTEROSAURS TO FLY.

HEAD

Anhanguera (which means "old devil") had an unusually large head. Skull fossils of this pterosaur show that it had bony rings in its eye sockets, like modern birds do. These may have given extra support to the eyes.

JAWS AND TEETH

This pterosaur's teeth were angled to catch and hold its fish prey, which it caught while skimming the surface of the water. The teeth were sharp, for piercing the fish's body, and curved to keep it from falling out of the pterosaur's mouth.

BALANCE

Some experts believe that this pterosaur flew with its head tilted to the side to keep its balance. They think this because fossils show that *Anhanguera* had an unusual inner ear structure, and this part of the body affects balance.

QUICK FACTS

PERIOD:
Early Cretaceous

LIVED IN:
South America

LENGTH:
4 feet (1.2 m)

WINGSPAN:
15 feet (4.6 m)

CREST

Anhanguera had a small crest at the back of its skull. It also had round crests at the front of its upper and lower jaws. These may have been for display or to communicate with other *Anhanguera*.

DINOMIGHTY!

The large eye sockets in *Anhanguera*'s skull suggest that it had big eyes and excellent eyesight–essential for spotting prey below while flying high in the sky.

TEETH AND BEAKS

ONE OF THE MAIN DIFFERENCES BETWEEN THE BASAL PTEROSAURS AND THE PTERODACTYLOIDS WAS THEIR TEETH. EARLY PTEROSAURS HAD LOTS OF TEETH. LATER SPECIES HAD LONGER BEAKS, BUT FEWER TEETH—SOMETIMES THEY HAD NONE AT ALL!

Dorygnathus had a "cage" of teeth that stuck out from its jaw to trap fish.

Basal pterosaurs usually had rows of sharp teeth in their upper and lower jaws. They used these to stab or grab fish and small prey. Some pterosaurs had a kind of "fringe" of closely packed teeth, which worked a bit like a sieve.

Pterosaur beaks came in different shapes and sizes. Some were long, and curved upward. These may have been used to dig for food in the seabed. Other pterosaurs had spoon-shaped beaks, which were good for scooping up and holding prey.

Dsungaripterus had a toothless, upwardly curved beak.

Different pterosaurs had different diets. Some ate fish. Others caught insects. Although young pterosaurs could fly, they may not have been able to catch their own food. A parent may have brought up food from its own stomach to feed the young reptile, a bit like modern birds.

Because most pterosaurs ate fish, they probably lived near water–seas, lakes, rivers, and swamps.

SORTED:

EUDIMORPHODON

SMALL *EUDIMORPHODON* WAS ONE OF THE EARLIEST PTEROSAURS. IT WAS UNUSUAL IN HAVING A MORE COMPLEX SET OF TEETH THAN MOST FLYING REPTILES.

QUICK FACTS

PERIOD:
Late Triassic

LIVED IN:
Europe

LENGTH:
2.3 feet (70 cm)

WINGSPAN:
3.3 feet (1 m)

DIET

Often experts have to guess what prehistoric animals ate. However, we know for sure what *Eudimorphodon* liked to eat because the remains of small, bony fish have been found inside fossils of this pterosaur. *Eudimorphodon* may have dived right under the water to catch fish, before surfacing again.

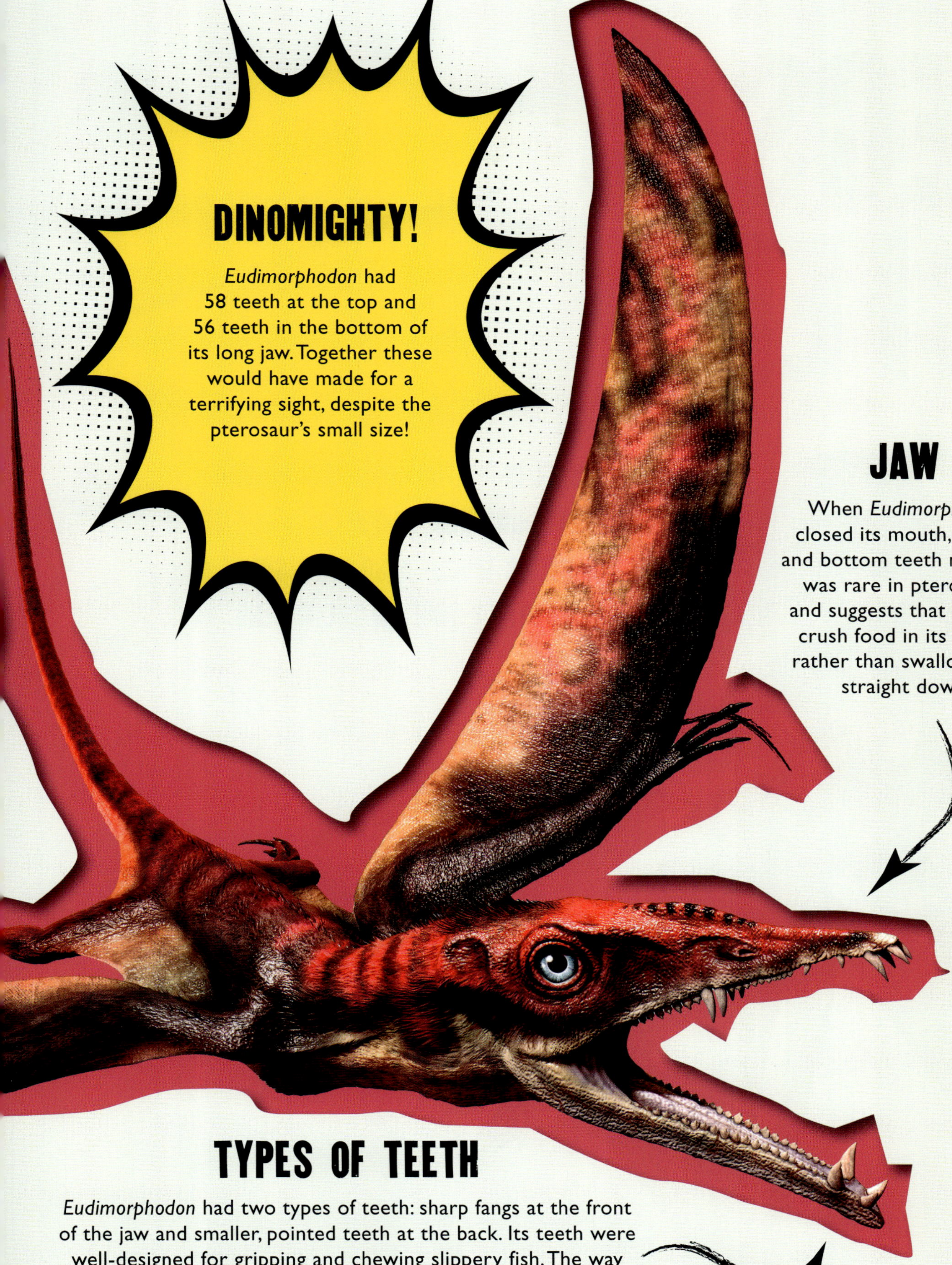

DINOMIGHTY!

Eudimorphodon had 58 teeth at the top and 56 teeth in the bottom of its long jaw. Together these would have made for a terrifying sight, despite the pterosaur's small size!

JAW

When *Eudimorphodon* closed its mouth, its top and bottom teeth met. This was rare in pterosaurs and suggests that it could crush food in its mouth rather than swallowing it straight down.

TYPES OF TEETH

Eudimorphodon had two types of teeth: sharp fangs at the front of the jaw and smaller, pointed teeth at the back. Its teeth were well-designed for gripping and chewing slippery fish. The way that some fossil teeth have been worn down suggests that *Eudimorphodon* also ate some hard-shelled invertebrates.

LEGS AND FEET

WHEN WE THINK OF PTEROSAURS, WE IMAGINE THEM SOARING THROUGH THE SKY. BUT THESE REPTILES WOULD ALSO HAVE SPENT A LOT OF TIME ON THE GROUND.

On land, pterosaurs would have been able to walk in a kind of upright position, using strong legs as back limbs. They folded their wings upward to create front legs, and used their first three fingers (see page 11) as front "feet."

◀ Pterosaurs like this *Zhejiangopterus* could walk effectively on all fours by manipulating their wings to become "legs." Tracks of pterosaur footprints show this unusual way of walking on land.

A pterosaur's back legs were quite large, with strong muscles able to launch them into the air. Because pterosaurs could also use their front "legs" to push off, this doubled their power for takeoff.

For a long time, experts thought that a pterosaur's legs splayed out toward the sides while it was flying. But recent research into the way that pterosaurs' ligaments were structured suggests that, in fact, their legs didn't bend that way. Their legs probably trailed directly behind their body.

The idea of legs hanging out to the side was based on how bats fly, but pterosaurs probably did not have the movement in their joints to allow this leg position.

SORTED:

DIMORPHODON

THIS EARLY PTEROSAUR HAD A BIG, DOME-SHAPED JAW AND SHARP TEETH FOR EATING ITS PREY OF FISH, LIZARDS, AND INSECTS. BUT ITS MOST UNUSUAL FEATURE WAS ITS LEGS!

QUICK FACTS

PERIOD:
Early Jurassic

LIVED IN:
Europe

LENGTH:
3.3 feet (1 m)

WINGSPAN:
4.6 feet (1.4 m)

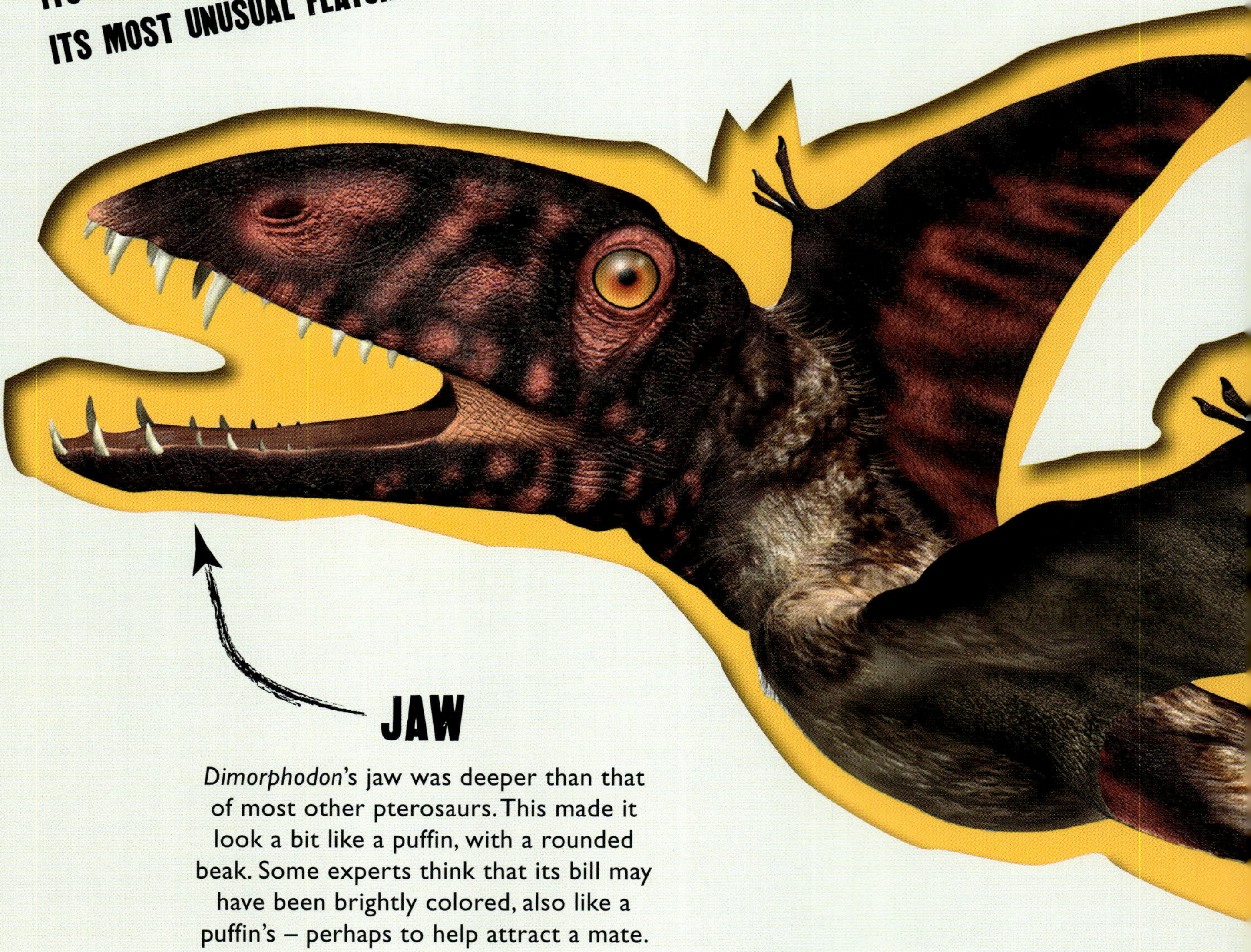

JAW

Dimorphodon's jaw was deeper than that of most other pterosaurs. This made it look a bit like a puffin, with a rounded beak. Some experts think that its bill may have been brightly colored, also like a puffin's – perhaps to help attract a mate.

DINOMIGHTY!

Dimorphodon's large skull has several wide openings. These were essential to reduce the weight of the pterosaur's head!

CLAWS

On its wings, *Dimorphodon* had strong claws. It used these to climb rocks or trees so that it could launch itself into the air to take flight. It may also have used these wing claws like front feet, so it could move aroung on all fours on the ground when it wasn't standing upright.

LEGS

Dimorphodon had unusually strong legs, which were much more developed than the legs on other known pterosaurs. Paleontologists think *Dimorphodon* may even have been able to walk upright, with its legs beneath its body.

GLOSSARY

AIR SACS – holes in the bones that reduce their weight

ANCESTOR – someone or something from the same family many generations earlier

ASTEROID – a large rock that forms in space and orbits the sun

CREST – a feature on the top of the head, made of bone, feathers, fur, or skin

EYE SOCKETS – the part of the skull that the eyeballs fit into

FOSSIL – the shape of a plant or animal that has been preserved in rock for a very long time

LIGAMENTS – strong, stringy tissue that connects bones in the body

MASS EXTINCTION – the death of many living things

MATE – a reproductive partner

MEMBRANE – a very thin layer of tissue covering parts of the body

NASAL PASSAGE – the channels that run inside the body from the nostrils

PALEONTOLOGIST – a scientist who studies dinosaurs and prehistoric life

PRESERVED – kept in good condition over a long period of time

PREY – animals that are hunted by other animals for food

SCAVENGER – an animal that feeds on dead animals rather than killing them itself

SKULL – the bones that make up the head and face

SPECIES – a group of living things that are closely related and share similar features

SUB-GROUP – a group of animals within a larger category that have particular features in common

VERTEBRAE – the bones that make up the spine, or backbone (singular: vertebra)

VERTEBRATE – an animal with a backbone inside its body

WINGSPAN – the length from the tip of one wing to the tip of the other

FURTHER INFORMATION

BOOKS

Children's Encyclopedia of Prehistoric Life
By Dougal Dixon (Arturua, 2024)

Pterosaur
By Lily Austen (Jump!, Inc., 2026)

Quetzalcoatlus
By Mary E. Bleckwehl (Black Rabbit Books, 2025)

DRAW YOUR OWN

Use the information in this book to design a new pterosaur species. Remember to include all the features of pterosaurs. Then give your reptile a name.

WEBSITES

www.amnh.org/exhibitions/pterosaurs-flight-in-the-age-of-dinosaurs/what-is-a-pterosaur
Find out more about pterosaurs from the American Museum of Natural History.

www.nhm.ac.uk/discover/watch-a-pterosaur-fly.html
Watch a pterosaur fly in this video from the Natural History Museum in the UK.

INDEX